The Life and Work of...

Claude Monet

Sean Connolly

Heinemann
LIBRARY

First published in Great Britain by
Heinemann Library,
Halley Court, Jordan Hill, Oxford OX2 8EJ
a division of Reed Educational and Professional
Publishing Ltd.
Heinemann is a registered trademark of Reed
Educational & Professional Publishing Ltd.

OXFORD MELBOURNE AUCKLAND
JOHANNESBURG BLANTYRE GABORONE
IBADAN PORTSMOUTH (NH) USA CHICAGO

Designed by Celia Floyd
Illustrations by Fiona Osbaldstone
Originated by Dot Gradations
Printed in Hong Kong/China

03 02 01 00 99
10 9 8 7 6 5 4 3 2 1

ISBN 0 431 09177 3

British Library Cataloguing in Publication Data

Connolly, Sean
   Life and work of Claude Monet
   1. Monet, Claude, 1840-1926 – Juvenile literature
   2. Painters – France – Biography – Juvenile literature
   3. Painting, Modern – 19th century – France –
   Juvenile literature
   4. Painting, French – Juvenile literature
   I. Title
   759.4

For more information about Heinemann Library
books, or to order, please telephone
+44(0)1865 888066, or send a fax to +441865 314091.
You can visit our web site at www.heinemann.co.uk

Acknowledgements

The Publishers would like to thank the following for
permission to reproduce photographs:

Page 4, Portrait photograph of Claude Monet in
front of the pictures 'Waterlilies' in his studio. Page
5, Claude Monet 'The Waterlilies - The Clouds',
Credit: The Bridgeman Art Library/Giraudon. Page
6, Le Harve, Credit: Bibliotheque Nationale. Page 7,
Claude Monet 'The coast of Normandy viewed
from Sainte-Adresse', Credit: The Fine Arts Museum
of San Francisco. Page 9, Claude Monet 'Caricature
of a young dandy with a monocle', Credit: Giraudon.
Page 11, Claude Monet 'Le Pave de Chailly', Credit:
Giraudon. Page 12, National Gallery, London,
Credit: Hulton Getty. Page 13, Claude Monet 'The
Thames below Westminster', Credit: The Bridgeman
Art Library/National Gallery. Page 14, Edouard
Manet 'Monet in his studio', Credit: AKG. Page 15,
Claude Monet 'Boulevard St Denis, Argenteuil, in
Winter', Credit: Richard Saltonstall/Museum of Fine
Arts, Boston. Page 16, Boulevard des Capucines,
Credit: Hulton Getty. Page 17, Claude Monet
'Impression, Sunrise', Credit: Giraudon. Page 19,
Claude Monet 'Entrance to the Village of Vetheuil',
Credit: Exley/Rosenthal. Page 21, Claude Monet
'Haystack at Giverny', Credit: The Bridgeman Art
Library/Hermitage. Page 23, Claude Monet 'The
Cap of Antibes, Mistral', Credit: AKG. Page 24,
Rouen Cathedral, Credit: Pix. Page 25, Claude
Monet 'Rouen Cathedral, Albany Tower, Early
Morning', Credit: Exley/Rosenthal. Page 26, Portrait
photograph of Claude Monet and his wife Alice, St
Mark's Square, Venice, Credit: Giraudon. Page 27,
Claude Monet 'Palazzo de Mula, Venice', Credit:
Exley/Rosenthal. Page 28, Photograph of Monet in
his garden, Credit: Corbis. Page 29, Claude Monet
'Waterlilies', Credit: Giraudon.

Cover photograph reproduced with permission of
Bridgeman Art Library

Our thanks to Paul Flux for his comments in the
preparation of this book.

Every effort has been made to contact copyright
holders of any material reproduced in this book.
Any omissions will be rectified in subsequent
printings if notice is given to the Publisher.

Any words appearing in the text in bold, **like this**,
are explained in the Glossary.

Contents

Who was Claude Monet?

Claude Monet was a French artist who was one
of the **Impressionists**. This group of painters tried
to show the change of light through the day
in their paintings.

4

Claude painted the same **scene** many times to show the change of light. This painting shows clouds **reflected** in the lily pond in his garden.

Early years

Claude Oscar Monet was born in Paris on 14 November 1840. His family soon moved to the **port** of Le Havre. Claude liked being near the sea.

Claude loved the way light showed on water.

This drawing shows the coast near Le Havre.

Claude drew it when he was 24 years old.

Schoolboy success

Claude did not like school. He made clever **caricatures** of his classmates. A local painter called Eugène Boudin saw these drawings. He wanted Claude to become a painter.

Claude could pick out the important bits to draw. He was 16 years old when he made this funny drawing of a young man dressed in stylish clothes.

Making friends

In 1861 Claude joined the army but became ill after a year. His family gave him some money to become a painter. Claude moved to Paris when he was 22 years old.

Claude became close friends with other young
artists in Paris. They often painted together.
Claude painted this **scene** on a trip to the
countryside near Paris.

Living in London

In 1870 Claude married Camille Doncieux. France was at war with Germany. Paris was dangerous so Claude and his wife moved to London. This is a picture of how London looked then.

Claude and his wife lived for a while in London.
Claude saw many paintings by English artists.
He painted the river Thames many times while
he was in London.

Discovering light

In 1871 Claude moved to Argenteuil, a small town near Paris. He built a floating **studio** to study how light affects water. This is a painting by Edouard Manet of Claude painting in his studio.

Claude liked to paint outside in every season. This painting shows a street in Argenteuil in the winter. He painted it in 1875.

Impressionism

Claude and his friends painted quickly. Most **galleries** thought their paintings looked messy. In 1874 the group **exhibited** their own paintings. The exhibition was in a building in this street.

The group became known as the **Impressionists**.
The name came from the title of this painting by
Claude called *Impression, Sunrise*. He had painted
a harbour just after **dawn**.

Two families

Claude and his family moved in with their friend Alice Hoschede and her children. Claude now had to look after two families and eight children.

Claude began painting around his new home in
Vétheuil. He used quick **strokes** of the brush to
show light and shape.

Giverny

In 1879 Camille died. In 1883 Claude and the two families moved to Giverny, near Paris. He loved his new garden. He also painted in the countryside near by.

Claude worked quickly. He began painting the same **scenes** over and over. This painting tells us about the houses, fields and even the weather one afternoon.

Painting trips

Claude spent many months away from home each year during the 1880s. He travelled around France and painted many **landscapes**. He worked in all sorts of weather.

This painting shows the seashore in the south of France. Claude used quick **brushwork**. We can almost feel the wind blowing through the trees and across the sea.

Series paintings

Claude kept painting the same **scenes** at different times. Together these pictures are known as his **series paintings**. He painted this **cathedral** at Rouen many times.

Claude loved to paint the front of Rouen Cathedral. It is almost hidden by mist in this picture. Other paintings show it in bright sunshine.

Travels

Claude made his last painting trips when he was over 60 years old. He went to Spain, Holland, England and Italy. This is a picture of Claude and Alice in Venice, Italy.

Claude loved the buildings in Venice. They rise straight out of the water. This painting shows a beautiful palace **reflected** in the water.

Waterlilies

Claude spent his last years at home in Giverny. He still thought about light and shape. He died aged 86 on 5 December 1926. The other **Impressionists** had died long before that.

Many of Claude's last works were huge paintings of waterlilies. In this painting it is hard to tell where the lilies end and their **reflections** begin.

Timeline

1840	Claude Monet born in Paris on 14 November, but soon moves to Le Havre.
1845	The artist Mary Cassatt is born.
1853	The artist Vincent van Gogh is born in Holland.
1857	Claude meets the painter Eugène Boudin.
1862	Claude moves to Paris to become a painter.
1865	American Civil War ends.
1865–6	Claude has paintings shown to the public in Paris.
1870	Claude marries Camille Doncieux and lives in London.
1870–71	War between France and Germany
1871	Claude moves to a new house in Argenteuil.
1874	Claude helps set up the first **exhibition** by the **Impressionists**.
1876	The telephone is invented.
1879	Camille dies. The artist Paul Klee is born in Switzerland.
1883	Claude moves to Giverny.
1890	The artist Vincent van Gogh dies.
1893	Claude begins work on building a pond in the garden at Giverny.
1898	The sculptor Henry Moore is born in England.
1906	The artist Paul Cézanne dies.
1909	First public showing of Claude's waterlily paintings.
1912	Claude develops an eye illness which slows his painting.
1914–18	The First World War is fought in Europe.
1926	Claude Monet dies on 5 December.

Glossary

brushwork   marks left by an artist's paint brush

caricature   funny drawing of someone

cathedral   large church

dawn   when it starts to get light in the morning

exhibit   display works of art

gallery   place where works of art are shown and sold

Impressionists   group of artists who painted outside to make colourful pictures

landscape   painting of the countryside

port   city on the edge of the ocean

reflect   give a second picture of something, as with a mirror

scene   place or area

series paintings   many paintings of the same subject but painted at different times

stroke   mark made by one movement of the brush

studio   special room or building where an artist works

More books to read

What Makes a Monet a Monet? New York: Metropolitan Museum of Art/Crabtree Books

Changing Colour, Looking at pictures, Joy Richardson, Franklin Watts

Tell me about Claude Monet, John Malam, Evans

More paintings to see

Poplars, Claude Monet, The Fitzwilliam Museum, Cambridge

Rouen Cathedral Façade, Claude Monet, National Museum of Wales, Cardiff

The Water Lily Pond, Claude Monet, National Gallery, London

Index